# Essential Oils For Pets Guide:

## Natural Remedies and Ailments, Aromatherapy Recipes For Cats, Dogs and Other Animals

By

Angela Pierce

# Table of Contents

Introduction .................................................................... 5

Chapter 1. About Essential Oils ...................................... 7

Chapter 2. Risks .............................................................. 10

Chapter 3. Benefits ......................................................... 14

Chapter 4. Dogs, Cats Other Pets .................................. 17

Chapter 5. Additional Recipes ....................................... 27

Final Words .................................................................... 29

Thank You Page .............................................................. 31

Essential Oils For Pets Guide: Natural Remedies and Ailments, Aromatherapy Recipes For Cats, Dogs and Other Animals

By Angela Pierce

© Copyright 2015 Angela Pierce

Reproduction or translation of any part of this work beyond that permitted by section 107 or 108 of the 1976 United States Copyright Act without permission of the copyright owner is unlawful. Requests for permission or further information should be addressed to the author.

This publication is designed to provide accurate and authoritative information in regard to the subject matter covered. This work is sold with the understanding that the publisher is not engaged in rendering legal, accounting, or other professional services. If legal advice or other expert assistance is required, the services of a competent professional person should be sought.

First Published, 2015

Printed in the United States of America

# Introduction

Anyone in touch with the 'alternative' wellbeing movement that is (finally) making headway in mainstream health, will be aware of something called 'essential oils'. You'll see them in cosmetics, moisturizers, shampoos, and soaps. They can be found as part of air freshening systems and detergents as well. You'll even see them added to foods, or occasional sold in your regular grocery store as nutritional supplements.

Use of essential oils, either aromatically, dermally, or internally, can be a highly effective, all natural way to achieve and maintain health; the same is true for your pets. Now, as is often the case, the rules for humans and the rules for your pets are not one and the same. Animals require special consideration due to their size, specific biological needs, and various other differences exhibited between species. Now, it's probably best to take your pet to the veterinarian if they exhibit symptoms of distress (many vets are beginning to utilize, recommend, and even sell oils specifically designed for pets),but with some research and knowledge, you can begin to treat your pet's basic needs at home by using essential oils.

## Chapter 1. About Essential Oils

In nature, all living things create some type of oil or wax. This is because life depends on water to exist, and therefore life must have some internal mechanism to hold, store, or isolate water within their bodies. Essential oils refer to the oils recovered from some living thing (most typically plants). Some plants produce a high volume of oil (think about olives) and others, far less (cinnamon). Lavender oil, for instance, requires about one-hundred pounds of raw plant material to produce 1 pound of mid-quality oil; good quality rose oil requires 8,000lbs. to make one pound of oil. The plant (or material) is typically heated or centrifuged to remove some excess water, and then pressed to extract the oils. The oils are then treated to remove additional water (water will destabilize the product as well as shorten its shelf life).

Essential oils can be made from nearly every part of the plant: Flowers, leaves, stems, bark, roots, rhizomes, seeds (nuts), or berries, fruits, pods, etc. Some parts of the plant contain only trace amounts of extremely potent oils, and these cannot be extracted through a simple mechanical process like described above. Instead, these oils are collected through some form of distillation. Gathering of these oils is a very labor intensive process, and the ultimate yields are extremely low. These oils are called 'absolute' (as in Chamomile Flower Absolute Essential Oil).

**Purchase**

There a few factors to consider when you begin to acquire your essential oil collection. Price, quality, producer, distributor, lot-numbers. Company reputation, intended use, personal recommendations, etc. In fact, if you are planning to use your oils for anything other than air freshener (for instance on you or your pet) then this is a process not to be taken lightly.

When shopping for oils to establish or add to your collection, purity and quality are what you need. First let's talk about purity. How pure is pure enough? Typically you want to go with 100% if you can afford it. This way you know exactly what you are using, you know there is no possibility of a contraindication due to an additive ingredient, and you get be certain of your dosages when mixing different oils to perform a certain function. The label on the bottle should read

"100% Pure xxx Oil". By the way, light can destabilize many sensitive compounds in your oils. They should always come in a dark green or dark brown, glass phial; this is just standard fare from any reputable company.

If you have to go with an option less than 100% purity, then the ingredients should be on the label. Often times, essential oils will be mixed with jojoba oil, olive or safflower oil, or some other adjutant oil. As long as you are familiar with these products, they can still be highly effective. Generally when an oil comes at less than 100% strength, it is a highly potent essential. In fact, many plant oils are harmful or even dangerous in their pure state. As long as you are using a reputable product, this adulterated oils can be absolutely fine.

Regardless Of whether you have 100% pure, or some diluted version, there are some things you will always expect to see on the bottles:

1) both the common name and scientific binomial name of the plant species
2) The company name and address
3) A batch or lot number for the product in that bottle
4) The origin of the botanical used in producing that oil

## Chapter 2. Risks

Personality wise, we like to think of our pets as very much like humans. At times it's undeniable, they seem to look, act, think, and feel as we do (except when they go nuts and we can't understand them at all...probably how they feel when wear formal dress). When it comes to nutrition, supplements, and use of EO (essential oils) you and your pet are not alike...not at all. Some extremely common oils used to treat human conditions can land your pet in the hospital or worse. Sometimes a slight overdose of a health EO can send them there as well. When it comes to birds and some exotics, you could kill them inadvertently while treating yourself. The point is, this should not be taken lightly. EO are powerful substances, and in many ways, your pets are far more sensitive than you or I.

**Common Killers**

There are many EOs that are beneficial to humans which can be devastating to your furry or feathered friends (slimy or scaly friends later). Though many of these are common for humans, the bodies or your animals may process them differently, or in the case of some, not process them at all. This can result in toxic organ failure, tachycardia, depressed nervous function, slowed breathing, and even death. For some of these oils, the plant itself is not toxic at all (basil is good for your dog if your dog likes it) but the extremely concentrated oil can be fatal (basil oil contains potentially hazardous phenylpropanoids).

There are two very common essential oil ingredients that can be harmful or even deadly for most non-human animals. The first one is something called 'pennyroyal'. It is an oil derived from one of three members of the Mentha family of herbs. It is often used in flea and tick treatments. You'll find it on the labels of large commercial brands, as well as in dependant company treatments. Pennyroyal is highly effective in killing and dissuading parasites, however it can be highly toxic. The problem with pennyroyal is that it is a cumulative toxin, or at least it can prove to be so. Studies have shown that over time, secondary chemical ingredient develops after absorption through skin, or ingestion by licking and grooming. This can accumulate in the body as most animals have no way to eliminate this toxin through normal processes. In dogs, this can lead to inflammatory disorders and stomach problems. In cats, which have very unique excretion systems, it can lead to kidney damage and non-reversible liver failure. This ingredient is best avoided, as it is not essential to effective treatments, and there are other alternatives on the market. It may not be listed on the front label, but you can find it in the ingredients listing.

Another often used but highly dangerous essential oil is tea tree. This has become a household item for many people as it's beneficial qualities are well known for humans. We use it to treat cuts, scrapes, abrasions, and rashes. Additionally, bad breath, mouth sores, hair treatments; the list goes on and on. Many pet product companies have begun listing tea tree as an ingredient. Fortunately it is often in concentrations so low as to have negligible impact on the product itself. Likely, this is just a ploy to attract the attention of the consumer that knows the health benefits of tea tree. If, however, a product were to contain significant amount of this oil, the results could be devastating to your pet. Tea tree is very powerful, and in studies it tends to effect other mammals far differently than it does humans. It can result in chemical burns, welting, sores, rash, digestive disorders, ataxia, and rapid heartbeat. Tea tree should always be avoided with your pet. If you treat yourself with tea tree oil, be certain that oil has been fully absorbed into your skin before contacting your pet.

## Chapter 3. Benefits

Now that we have established the risks involved with EO and animals, and we understand what it takes to make safe informed purchases of high quality oils for use on you and your pets (that's one nice benefit...no need for separate medicine chests) let's talk briefly about the benefits of using essential oils. Briefly, because we could spend days discussing the possibilities of improving and prolonging the life of the animals you love whether they be a dormouse, a dachshund, or a Clydesdale.

**Calm**

Aromatic oils can be used effectively to create a calming environment for your pet. This can be beneficial when preparing to travel, receive company, or take a trip to the vet's office. One simple way to apply calming agents such as lavender or bergamot, is to prepare a simple sachet. Mix the oils of your choice and dilute slightly with olive oil or jojoba (essentially an oil with little fragrance). Next, take some sawdust, wood shavings, or even small animal bedding (not cedar) and thoroughly mix the oils into the shavings.

Wrap the shavings in a porous cloth like cheesecloth or even a cotton bandanna and tie securely. This sachet can be hung near (not in) an animal's environment. For example, you can hang it outside a bird's cage, a rabbit hutch or a guinea pig house. If you have a cat or small dog, you can place the sachet in the travel case 20 minutes prior to travel, and then remove it before your pet goes in the box. For large dogs, you can hold and pet them while exposing them to the oils and let them decide how much is enough.

**Coat and Skin**

There are many oils appropriate for adding lustre and shine to your animal's coat, and for improving skin quality, and remedying skin conditions like eczema and rash. As always, with lesions or other compromised skin, it's best to consult a professional, as the results of dermal application can vary widely from direct exposure to the bloodstream.

**Teeth and Breath**

Many oils can be added to food or water dishes to improve dental health and create fresher breath (especially in dogs). Likewise, for small animals, tiny quantities of an oil can be diluted in an entire water bottle for effective dosage. Small animals can be treated very effectively with EO, but the application methods must take into account their size and sensitivity (more on that later).

## Chapter 4. Dogs, Cats Other Pets

Whichever animal you have in your home and in your heart, there are ways to incorporate EO into your life together, that can improve the quality of life you share. Let's take a look group by group and see what we can learn about EO and animals.

**Cats**

While cats have uniquely sensitive excretion systems (not nearly as robust as a human or dog) they can still benefit greatly from the correct essential oils boost. Proper oils can aide in digestion, the elimination of hairballs, promote healthier skin and coat, improve natural defenses against infection, and help to dissuade fleas, ticks, and other parasites from choosing your kitty as their new home. Some oils that are safe and effective for cats include: Copaiba (Copaifera officinalis), Thyme (Thymus vulgaris), Basil (Ocimum basilicum), Frankincense (Boswellia carterii), Marjoram (Origanum majorana), Catnip (Nepeta cataria), Lavender (Lavandula angustifolia), Peppermint (Mentha piperita), Cypress (Cupressus sempervirens), Fennel(Foeniculum vulgare) and the Oregano (Origanum vulgare).

When applying oils to your cat (externally is the safest) you can simply drip 3-6 drops on their coat and stroke them until well dispersed. You may want to rub 'against the grain' in order to better work the oils deeper in. Now, if you know cats, you realize that it's inevitable that eventually the cat will clean itself and the oils will end up being taken internally. This is why it is important for you to work the oil as much as possible during the petting phase of application. By the time your cat begins to ingest the oil through cleaning behaviors, the oils should be sufficiently dispersed so as to prove no risk to your feline.

*Dry Skin (Dandruff)-* 1 part Bergemot, 1 part Ginger, 1 part Alder, 1 part Cedar

This is a nice combination for relieving dry, itchy, or flaky skin. Additionally, it has the effect of eliminating odors in older cats.

*Hairball Maintenance-* 1 part Patchouli, 1 part Sweet Almond, mix in cod liver oil at 5:1

Apply this directly to your cat's food or in their water (if they'll tolerate it) If you notice no signs of complication, continue to administer daily.

**Dogs**

Dogs test as the most robust when it comes to tolerating essential oils. This, of course, does not mean that you can assume them to be the same as a human. Even large dogs react differently to essential oils (because they are a different species) than humans do. Always use a very small amount of a substance and watch carefully for any negative behavioral changes. Fortunately, most dogs enjoy being petted and brushed. To apply an oil externally, brush first to remove excess hair. Then, applying the oil to your fingertips, slowly work it into the coat. It is important that the oil eventually reach the skin, for absorption. To accomplish this, it often works well to stroke the animal against the grain (direction of hair growth). Your dog will likely lick some of the oil off, but if diluted (as it should be) this will not cause any harm. That's one of the benefits of using high quality natural ingredients. When administering oils internally, never put full strength oils in your dog's mouth, they can burn. Add oil to foods a few drops per feeding. In low concentrations, even a picky animal shouldn't mind. Some oils that are safe and effective for dogs include: Copaiba (Copaiba officinalis), Helichrysum (H. italicum), Peppermint (Mentha piperita), as well as all the normal digestive oils like those of parsley, lemongrass, wheatgrass, barley, and Chrysanthemum.

*Paws-* 2 parts Yarrow, 1 part Bitter Almond, 1 part Ginger, 1 part Thyme  -mix in coconut or jojoba
This recipe can be applied liberally at any time.

*Ear Care-* 1 part Hyssop, 1 part Spruce, 1 part Lemon, 1 part Eucalyptus
This is ideal for soothing the effects of ear mites and other ear discomfort, and may prevent additional infestation

*Calm-* 1 part Lavender, 1 part Tarragon, 1 part Frankincense

*Indigestion-* 1 part Parsley, 1 part Chamomile, 1 part Cedar, 1 part Fennel

**Birds**

Now, through your research, you'll read a lot of controversy about birds and EO. Basically, birds are far more sensitive to VOC (volatile organic compounds) than one might suspect. As such, even burning the wrong scented candle in too close proximity to certain birds can result in nothing short of death. For this reason, many 'experts' have taken to blanket warnings forbidding the use of any essential oil on or near any bird at any time. This type of knee-jerk reaction only serves to misinform the public (who are seeking truthful and well researched information) and also denies bird owners a terrific tool in improving the life of their bird.

Now it is true that birds can suffer greatly from the misuse of botanicals, and that even an incidental exposure can prove deadly. But that doesn't mean that thoughtful, careful application of the correct materials at the correct dilutions cannot be advantageous to them. Rather it just reminds us that these materials are not to be considered lightly (including in application to ourselves).

Now, not all birds like to be petted, and even those that do spend a good part of their time preening. Additionally, oils applied to feathers can result in the buildup of dust and dirt and contribute to ill effects. Most experts (real experts) who recommend EO for birds say that you should purchase a diffuser. This is a simple machine that aerosolized the oil droplets while mixing them with water and sending a mist into a small surrounding area. This method is pleasant because both you and your bird can enjoy the results as you breath the common air infused with whatever agent you are applying at that time.

Some favorites for birds include:
Rosemary (Rosmarinus officinalis),
Cinnamon (Cinnamomum zeylanicum), Lemon (Citrus limon), Spruce (Picea mariana), Eucalyptus, Clove(Eugenia caryophyllata), Frankincense(Boswellia carterii), Copaiba (Copaifera officinalis),
Marjoram (Origanum majorana), and also the Tangerine (Citrus reticulate).

Notice that many of the oils healthful to birds, would make your dog severely ill, and might kill a cat (spruce, eucalyptus, cinnamon) depending on potency and dose. This again goes to illustrate how subtle an art EO can be when it come to animals. I say this again, not to dissuade you, but to encourage you to become informed.

*Feather Sheen-* 1 part Lavender, 1 part Bitter Orange, 1 part Lemon, 1 part Frankencense

Mix thoroughly and add to a spray bottle. Mist your bird one-to-several times per week as needed. You should notice a luster and fullness to your bird's plumage within 4 applications.

*Digestion-* 1 part hempseed, 1 part Bergamot, 1 part Fennel, 1 part Anise

This mixture can be added, 1 drop for small birds, 3 drops for larger species like macaws, directly to their food dish.

*Mite Inhibitor-* 1 part Cedar, 1 part Yew, 1 part Lemongrass

Drip this mixture, undiluted on the back of head and neck and allow it to naturally diffuse across the bird's feathers. This can help remove mites, and inhibit future infestations

## Small Animals

While small animals are delicate in many regards, with appropriate dosage, they will benefit from EO as much as you or your dog and cat. There are some special consideration when considering some small animals. Rabbits and Guinea pigs, for example, have complex and sensitive digestive tracts. For this reason, strong oils, or those with anti-microbial properties should not be used. Ferrets have active sebaceous (oil producing) glands, and therefore misting, or water infusion might be a better way to administer healthful dosages. Additionally, there are some special application techniques to use with your small animals that work specifically just for them (and will be fun for you)

Chinchillas have extremely sensitive skin. Not sensitive in that it necessarily overreacts to stimuli, but rather that its integument serves to integrate the external environment readily. This is due, in part, to the fact that they have more hair follicles than any other land mammal. So, external application of EO to the fur of a chinchilla may be too intense for the little critter. Additionally, it may actually clog hair follicles, leading to skin disorders. They maintain a highly sensitive balance (in captivity) as any chinchilla owner knows. Rather than an external application, it's best to provide an ingestible application.

One method of ingestion, for any small animal, is through dilution in a water bottle.  Most small animals do not balk at EO in their drinking water, and this can provide a long-term low-dose application.  This is also a great way to provide essential oils to this animals that may be less gregarious or do not enjoy petting. Another method, and this is sweet and fun for you both, is to apply a bit of the essential oil directly to your hand (use the back of your hand, as we want your skin to absorb the oil).  Wait until the oil is fully absorbed (no more shiny spot) and then allow your little critter to lick and kiss that spot.  Being such very small little animals, and the oil as intense as it is, most times your animal will notice the area and naturally pursue the oil on their own.  Small animals, having such intense nutritional needs, have developed an uncanny sensitivity towards anything beneficial to them.  That's why this secondary ingestion method is so effective, and fun!

Some essential oils that will benefit your small animal's skin, digestion, and overall health can include:
Lemon (Citrus limonum), Marjoram (Origanum majorana), Tangerine (Citrus tangerina),
Ginger (Zingiber officinalis), Anise(Pimpinella anisum), Peppermint (Mentha piperita), Fennel (Foeniculum vulgare), Basil (Ocimum basilicum),
Tarragon (Artemisia dracunculus), Juniper (Juniperus communis), and Patchouli (Pogostemon cablin.

Notice that these have a warming, earthy quality to them. Some practitioners are trying to establish families of botanicals in order to better which might work best for which conditions and which animals. Truly, as the field grows, we should see some wonderful discoveries.

*Rabbit & Guinea Pig Digestion-* 2 parts Oregano, 1 part Sassafras, 1 part Patchouli
This can be administered via water bottle at 3-7 drops per bottle. The effects should be seen within 2 days.

*Chinchilla Ear Health-* 1 part Lavender, 1 part Chamomile, 1 part Cedar, 1 part Sweet Almond

## Chapter 5. Additional Recipes

*Deodorizing* - Use this recipe and diffuse into the main room or area of odor concentration. Believe it or not, this is even effective for a 'ferret room'. If it works there, it will certainly work to counter a litter box or dog bed.

2 Parts Sage, 2 Parts Yew, 1 Part Eucalyptus, 1 Part Cedar

*Refreshing* - This can be diffused for small animals and birds (always dilute and use caution for birds) It can be used to enliven your pets and your whole home. Additionally, This recipe promotes healthy skin.

2 Parts Bitter Orange, 1 Part Camphor, 1 Part Rosemary, 1 Part Spearmint

*Shine* - This is equally effective on birds or furry animals. It promotes skin health and production of healthy fur/feathers. You'll notice an improvement to your skin and hair as well if you diffuse this into your home once or twice a week.

1 Part Rose, 1 Part Grapefruit, 1 Part Russian Violet, 1 Part Oregano

*Insect Control* - This formula will help deter insects if diffused into your home. When applied directly to your animal's coat, it will help prevent infestation and even chase off the bugs already hiding there. With smaller and more sensitive animals, be certain to properly dilute the formula in a carrier oil such as jojoba or coconut. The effects occur once the oil is absorbed into the skin, not merely upon application. Watch for signs of irritation as some pets can be sensitive to this mixture. Others will love its invigorating effects.

2 Parts Citronella,1 Part Lemongrass, 1 Part Thyme,1 Part Camphor

Apply this oil to areas not easily licked by your pet. It is very strong until it is absorbed.

## Final Words

The biggest risk to pets is an uneducated caregiver. It is necessary to learn about essential oils before you begin administering them to your pet. Some oils are good for one animal and not another. Read forums and message boards online to get a sense of the potential complications you may face. Always watch your animal closely when administering a new brand, new batch, or new combination of oils. Watch their breathing, their pupils, their behavior. With cats be aware of new smells, or listlessness, as it may be a sign that the oils are affecting organ function.

Always take it slow when finding the right dosage. Begin with the smallest amount you can realistically administer, and work up from there. With essential oils, your goal should be to establish balance and long term health. As such, it's best to apply lower doses over prolonged periods of time. This is especially true when the oil is being taken internally. Remember that these are extremely potent, and even oils absorbed through the skin will have a powerful effect on the organism as a whole (also true for you when applying the oils)

If you are treating a skin problem, its best to cut your oil with something soothing, like shea butter or cocoa butter.  This will prevent the oils from exacerbating a sensitive condition, and allow them to do their work without harming the sensitive tissue.

## Thank You Page

I want to personally thank you for reading my book. I hope you found information in this book useful and I would be very grateful if you could leave your honest review about this book. I certainly want to thank you in advance for doing this.

If you have the time, you can check my other books too.

www.ingramcontent.com/pod-product-compliance
Lightning Source LLC
LaVergne TN
LVHW021746060526
838200LV00052B/3510